# Quarantined With My Coworkers

*145 bizarre, ridiculous, and funny things they did during COVID-19*

Copyright © 2020 by Mike Stoupa
All rights reserved

No part of this publication may be reproduced, distributed, or transmitted in any form or by any means, including photocopying, recording, or other electronic or mechanical methods, or by any information storage and retrieval system without the prior written permission of the publisher, except in the case of very brief quotations embodied in reviews and certain noncommercial uses permitted by law.

# Your free bookmark is waiting!

Have you ever walked around the corner at your office and thought, "What was I walking over here to do?" Well, I will not be able to help you with your short-term memory but my colleagues are happy to help you remember your place in a book!

Created by the two main characters in this book, and I use the term 'characters' loosely, these employees painstakingly crafted numerous works of art for you to enjoy. To receive one of these free hand-drawn bookmarks, fill out the short form on this page: www.tinyurl.com/QuarantinedBookmark. I am happy to mail it to a friend, that colleague who chews entirely too loud, your archnemesis in the Sales department, or your Aunt Carol, who is a big fan of yours.

No purchase necessary to receive the bookmark. Please know that, when you buy a book in this series, you are helping support charities doing good work in their community!

# Table of Contents

| | |
|---|---|
| **Introduction To My Savage Coworkers** | 1 |
| April 2020 | 4 |
| May 2020 | 16 |
| June 2020 | 30 |
| July 2020 | 41 |
| August 2020 | 55 |
| September 2020 | 71 |
| **Note of Encouragement** | 81 |
| **Special Thanks** | 82 |
| **About the Author** | 83 |

# My coworkers are savage.

# Admit yours are too!

If you are reading this, you have someone you work with who is on the crazy spectrum.

We all complain about them in private but are often too scared to share their antics outside our inner circle of trusted friends. I am here to free you of your burden by publicly sharing the annoying, petty, obscure, and downright hilarious antics of my coworkers during the COVID-19 pandemic.

Without fear of retribution, I am also going to share a secret about why the actions of my coworkers will never get them fired.

*Enjoy the magical ride to crazy town!*

# #mycoworkers

One day after I started working from home full-time in March 2020, I was doing what most of us were doing to pass the time: scrolling through Facebook.

I saw someone's idea to document all the ridiculous, out-of-line, and inappropriate things your pets do that would never be allowed or accepted in an office setting. Thinking it would give my friends, family, and colleagues something to laugh and smile about as a distraction from the chaos the COVID-19 pandemic was causing, I decided to do just that but with a slight twist.

Everything documented in this book is a true story of something they said or did. I only added embellishments around the backstory of how it relates to something your in-office colleagues would do, hopefully not do, or need to be reminded about.

There is one tiny, rather insignificant, almost minuscule, detail I should probably share before you dive into these humorous snippets of the over six months of quarantined corporate life. It is the kind of information that if you did not have in the beginning then you may wonder whether I should have sought out professional medical help for staying in the same job for so long. There is no debating that my coworkers truly are savages and probably should have been let go for their behavior long before the pandemic hit.

Remember that secret to lifetime employment I promised to tell you? Here's why, despite their best and worst efforts, my coworkers were not fired:

**My coworkers were my five-year-old son and two-year-old daughter.**

 Buckle up…

### April 3, 2020

My coworker just told me the paper was not working and proceeded to throw a tantrum in the break room. HR's suggestion: verbal warning.

#lifewithkids #givethemsnacks #daddydaycare #mycoworkers

### April 7, 2020

We are not 5 minutes into our morning shift and one coworker is already licking a bouncing ball and the other is crawling inside a bookshelf. HR's recommendation: sanitize frequently touched surfaces with a one-on-one discussion about expected behavior in the workplace, pursuant to policy 42.1.b.

#icantmakethisstuffup #8morehours #daddydaycare #mycoworkers

### April 8, 2020

During our break in the lunchroom, one of my coworkers put one hand on his hip and, in the sassiest tone possible, cocked eyebrow and all, said, "Is that really necessary Missy?!", to another coworker who was blowing raspberries at him over her disapproval of the lunch break ending. The best part was that he finished their conversation with, "Well, no cookies for you this afternoon!" I do not even know I should report this to HR...

#cookieswereavailable #daddydaycare
#mycoworkers

### April 9, 2020

In today's "I did not read the memo" update, one of my coworkers put himself in the oven in the break room to remain socially distant from another coworker who was pestering him about riding a rocking horse. HR said the horse was fair game but 6 feet is still 6 feet.

#itwasatoyoven #daddydaycare #mycoworkers

## April 10, 2020

With productivity clearly on the decline, two coworkers took it upon themselves to stick their heads in a large mixing bowl just to hear the echo sound it made when they yelled into it. A management meeting was called and it was decided that both team members should be reassigned to a different project in order to maintain the required output.

#noonewasletgo #isitnaptimeyet #daddydaycare #mycoworkers

## April 12, 2020

My coworkers showed up unannounced and insisted we work all weekend. When I informed them that budget cutbacks meant no overtime would be assigned, they brought in representation. After intense negotiations for what seemed like minutes, we agreed they would receive an Easter bonus instead of their regular paycheck. Shout out to the finance team for the advanced planning.

#easterbasketsforthewin #managementdeservestimeofftoo #daddydaycare #mycoworkers

## April 13, 2020

During our morning huddle, while I was providing guidance on this morning's projects, one of my coworkers stopped me mid-sentence by shouting my name. In a very stubborn tone, he proclaimed to the entire team, " I want to be a ninja!" Reminding him that, despite the COVID-19 pandemic, OSHA standards still apply, he gave me a lengthy story about how ninjas did not need socks and he would go around barefoot all day. After a verbal warning to comply, he reluctantly agreed and all team members left the meeting wondering if he would make it through the day without being let go.

#cantfirefamily #socksforsafety #daddydaycare #mycoworkers

## April 13, 2020

While working on a storyboard for an upcoming marketing campaign, one of my coworkers decided she was done and just decided to eat the paper she was working on. One coworker showed concern and brought it to her attention but she just smiled at him and swallowed, sticking her tongue out to prove she knew exactly what she had done. Distraught, the rest of the team ended the brainstorming session and broke for lunch. HR recommended personal counseling but, with the current backlog of paperwork HR is dealing with, I am unsure she'll get the help she needs before her current contract is up.

#itwaspeasize #gotmostofitout #daddydaycare #mycoworkers

## April 14, 2020

I am trying something different to motivate the team: having a dance party during our planning session. Just like with any new initiative, it was met with resounding delight at first. However, by the second song into the Frozen movie soundtrack, one coworker was tossing a stuffed Pikachu at the ceiling and another was literally biting the strings on the blinds.

There was mild success with playing some hits from All Time Low but overall productivity has not increased today. May have to go back to the drawing board about what motivates the team before I attempt a second round of this whole motivation thing. Ideas welcomed...

#bailmeoutforthewin #itsacatchysong #daddydaycare #mycoworkers

### April 15, 2020

I want to first state that there was no altercation or conflict to cause this but one of my coworkers lost a tooth. Does anyone have the contract terms for Tooth Fairy LLC? What is the 2020 rate? I sifted through all my files and they were all from the 1990s.

#firsttooth #wigglewigglegone #5dollarsseemswaytoohigh

### April 15, 2020

In the span of 20 seconds, my coworker said and did the following during our pre-shift water cooler discussion:
- "Why are you wearing a Valentine's shirt?"
- "I wish I lived in the land of food."
- "I do not need to wear underwear today."
- Taking his shirt off and then wearing it as a hat, "How do I look?!"
- While laying down on the floor with his neck angled so he could look behind him, "Why is everything upside down?"

A member of the HR team just sat there and watched it happen. If this lack of policy enforcement continues, I may have to send a memo to corporate.

#itwasavaisforloversshirt #daddydaycare #mycoworkers

### April 16, 2020

As the saga of sassy coworkers continues, one of my coworkers put a lounge chair on top of a rocking chair (we are one of those progressive causal offices). When instructed to return the office furniture to its proper place, he proclaimed, "I am the queen! Queens must sit in big chairs and this is now a big chair! Now, do you want to visit the queen?" Baffled by the whole ordeal, I attempted to deflect the situation by offering to have a pre-shift tea party. Since behavior returned to normal, no incident report was filed with HR. Our risk department, on the other hand, may have to get involved.

#whatwouldOSHAdo #sassyMcSasserton #daddydaycare #mycoworkers

### April 17, 2020

One of my coworkers, who obviously has a good understanding of the English language, is insisting our office is "H-Cube." When I tried to ask if he meant HQ, his reply was a simple facial expression that made it seem like I had been transported from an alternate dimension with six eyes and pentagons for ears.

In equally perplexing news, another coworker was having breakfast with me, saw my yogurt, and kept opening and closing her mouth as if she was a baby bird. I think she wanted a bite but not sure if it was some weird kind of "welcome to work" ritual. Just glad I did not have to talk to HR because they were giving me some serious side-eye action at the water cooler...

#toocomfortablewithyourcoworkers #dotheyevertakePTO #daddydaycare #mycoworkers

### April 17, 2020

Anyone's coworker ever have an epic breakdown during a staff meeting because their oversized stuffed Elmo wouldn't stay buckled in a stroller? Asking for a friend...

#itsthatkindofday #sendherhomeordealwithit #daddydaycare

#mycoworkers

## April 18, 2020

My job description definitely says upper management but these coworkers of mine must think I am a temporary contract worker by the way they defy instruction and constructive feedback. On at least 17 occasions, I had to remind two of them that rolling yourself into a taquito with the rug in the break room is not acceptable behavior. The only reason I am not writing them up formally is that they're technically not supposed to be here since it is the weekend. They are both on thin ice though. Yesterday, as I was wrapping up a team conference call, one started wrestling another while on the lounge seats. Upset about the whole situation, the other coworker responds by spanking the offending wrestler and yells, "I am going to bite your butt!" Because you are thinking it, of course, I was not on mute.

#everyoneheardit #laughedsohardtheycried #iwasnotasmused #daddydaycare #mycoworkers

## April 19, 2020

Thankfully today was fairly uneventful at the office so my end-of-shift report was short. However, I did have to scratch my head a little when one of my coworkers was conducting the annual physical inventory of his cubicle. I asked for the final tally and he shared this observation, which clearly lacked backup documentation: "2 + 4 = Domino's". It was then I knew we had to do an audit of the past 4+ years he's been employed here.

#hewasserious #yethecancountto50 #maybehewashungry #daddydaycare #mycoworkers

### April 20, 2020

Hopefully this is not a foreshadowing of how the rest of the day will go. One coworker started his shift by trying to motivate himself by smacking himself in the face with a silicone pot holder. Another was sticking open markers in her mouth.

Please send prayers for me...

#theywerenontoxic #worriedlevel9 #daddydaycare #mycoworkers

### April 20, 2020

When one of your coworkers runs down the hall yelling "Zoom! Zoom!", you wonder for a split second whether he is really late to a video conference call or running from some mythical beast he concocted a minute ago to justify leaving early for the day.

P.S. I did have to remind one female coworker that licking the table was not a sanitary way to eat her work-provided meal so there's that...

#mythicalbeastwasmommy #hygieneisasuggestion #daddydaycare #mycoworkers

### April 21, 2020

One of my coworkers said the following this morning prior to our 15-minute power walk break: "I am going to go outside and move like a shoe!"

Good luck with that buddy...

#healreadyhadshoeson #iwishiwaskidding #daddydaycare #mycoworkers

## April 21, 2020

Does anyone else have that coworker who constantly needs something, especially when you are in the middle of doing something important or not in the mood to deal with people? I have been dealt a pair of said type of coworker.

While having lunch, one asked for something and I told him he had to wait. Showing his impatience, he replied with this gem: "Well, I am gonna spank your heinie!"

The other one just smiled at me with an ear-to-ear grin...and then asked for more cheese.

#areyouthatcoworker #girllovescheese #daddydaycare #mycoworkers

## April 22, 2020

Going to try a new productivity booster policy: the afternoon siesta. One coworker felt it was a good addition to the daily routine and decided to take me up on it right away. The other is naturally rebellious from the start. So, when I entered the break room, I found him sitting upside down on the couch (feet pointing at the ceiling and head close to the ground) and from his mouth I see, hanging like a recently hunted prey from the Serengeti, a stuffed Pikachu.

#ihadthelastlaugh #hetookasiestatoo #iwonttellifyoujoinedthem #daddydaycare #mycoworkers

Here is photographic evidence. The items scattered throughout the picture tell you everything you need to know about what life at our office is like.

### April 23, 2020

In today's magical "I do not want to work" update, my coworkers had a sword fight with drumsticks and tried to poke each other in the stomach, in what looked like some sort of hierarchical establishing charade. One is now sitting in a crib playing with talking/singing race cars and the other is pretending to be a member of an elite robot force known as the Transformers. They have made it abundantly clear they give no cares about being productive at all today. Should I call their emergency contact on file to discuss the possible need for behavioral support? Or leave it to upper management to handle when they return later today? I am not playing their game to try to obtain a workaround to worker's compensation laws.

#thoughtweweremakingprogress #timeforlunch #daddydaycare #mycoworkers

### April 23, 2020

I was today years old when I learned, from one of our most senior front-line employees, that teeth are not called teeth anymore.

According to him, they are now called carrot cutters.

#keepingyouinformed #newfavoriteveggie #daddydaycare #mycoworkers

### April 24, 2020

Well, this productivity train took a hard left turn at Hellnoville and stopped at Screw This Junction. I caught one coworker climbing into a side table in her cubicle while another was head butting her butt. When I confronted him about the offense, he said, "But she likes it!" I signed him up for harassment training immediately. Please send any peanut butter treats to try to ease the headaches these two are causing. Tylenol is not cutting it anymore.

#strugglebus #PIPintheworks #daddydaycare #mycoworkers

### April 25, 2020

Ever have one of those no pants on, wear swimming goggles around the office because you can, throw a tantrum because you couldn't get access to a cleaning wipe kind of day at the office? My coworkers did...

#noovertime #supercasual #daddydaycare #mycoworkers

### April 26, 2020

During our morning break, I was heading towards my cubicle when I heard one of my coworkers talking with his supervisor:

Coworker: Hey, do you want to do yoga with me today?!
Supervisor: Yeah!
Coworker: Because I do not.

While his supervisor had an expressionless face, you could tell she was done with his attitude.

#nailedit #ilaughedtoo #daddydayvare #mycoworkers

## April 27, 2020

I witnessed some poor driving by one of my coworkers today and had to report it to the safety department. Saw him driving his red, yellow, and white vehicle with illegal sirens on the hood (looked like a mini fire truck based on the paint job), swerving between both sides of the unmarked street. He was clearly not paying attention as he almost drifted into a few parked cars. Probably should've performed a field sobriety test but no evidence to suggest the impaired operation of a vehicle. The passenger in the vehicle was also seen getting whiplash on at least 4 occasions. For those who are wondering, the vehicle was an automatic but he drove it like a new driver taking a manual transmission out for his first joy ride.

#theyweregoodtoday #wishfulthinkingfortomorrow #daddydaycare #mycoworkers

## April 28, 2020

Received this voice memo from a co-worker this morning and it needs no additional explanation: "You may not like this but I want to invite the Ninja Turtles over for dinner. But first, we have to trap them in our ball pit when they get here. Then we can let them go in our house for pizza on Friday. We can let them go back to their Sensei, Splinter, on Sunday."

Yes, we have a ball pit for creative breaks.

#clickclickdeleted #kidnappingisnotokay #thankfullynotreal #daddydaycare #mycoworkers

## April 29, 2020

For the past two days, our VP of Human Resources and I have cleaned up the clutter left on the floor in one of our coworker's cubicles. It was creating a walking hazard and would not have passed an OSHA audit. We simply moved it to a less obstructive location nearby. When said employee returned to work each day, he enthusiastically told us the Teenage Mutant Ninja Turtles had come to visit the office overnight. After realizing the clutter we moved were TMNT action figures and his productivity increased as a result, we are at a crossroads about whether to tell him they did not actually visit or to let it ride. Now I know what parents who do the Elf on a Shelf feel like. I am starting to get concerned about the well-being of this employee's roommates for having to put up with this guy daily.

#shouteddownthedraintosplinter #notkiddingaboutsplinter #daddydaycare #mycoworkers

## April 30, 2020

I was having a philosophical discussion with my coworker about the solar system and our life on Earth. When we discussed the other planets, I had to inform him that Jupiter had stripes of tan, brown, and a little bit of orange and yellow. He got irate and yelled, "Jupiter is red!" Even pictures from NASA did not convince him.

#confusedwithmars #nofakenewshere #daddydaycare #mycoworkers

## April 30, 2020

One coworker was chasing another down the hall shouting, "Criminal! Criminal! Get back here!" When I heard the commotion, curiosity got the best of me so I followed the noise to investigate. To my surprise, the coworker who was yelling stood in front of the storage closet in his cubicle, rear-end holding it closed. When I asked him what he was doing, he said it was jail. I opened the door to find another coworker trapped inside, giggling at the ridiculousness of the situation. I did not report the incident to upper management because it seemed to be a game they were playing to spark creativity. Maybe it is time to order some stress relievers for the office...

#officekidnapping #noonewasharmed #bakedgoodsneededtosurvive #daddydaycare #mycoworkers

## April 30, 2020

Anyone working with normal people: Hey! How's your day going?!

Me: Hanging in there. My coworker tried to eat Play-Doh. How's your day going?

#shespititout #isitquittingtimeyet #daddydaycare #mycoworkers

## May 1, 2020

I swear these coworkers of mine do not read the company-wide memos on health and hygiene we distribute daily. One tried to eat the buttons on her jacket during our morning power walk and also was seen licking/biting the carpeted stairs going to the second-floor executive offices. Another was witnessed sticking his head in a culvert pipe while trying to find his friend Raphael the turtle. Hand washing procedures have since been thoroughly reviewed with in-person training and both are now required to have supervised sanitation breaks.

#dirtdoesntbuildcharacter #soapsaves #daddydaycare #mycoworkers

## May 2, 2020

I had a discussion with my coworkers about things we wished for during this pandemic. Here were their insights:

VP of Human Resources: I wish this pandemic would end.
Me: I wish we could go on vacation.
Newly hired associate: Dat! dat! *pointing to a muffin which she did not end up eating*
Senior entertainment associate: I wish I could run through my ears.

#muffinsaregoodwishes #wewonderabouthimsometimes #daddydaycare #mycoworkers

## May 3, 2020

Senior entertainment associate: Do you want to play the monster game?
Me: How do you play the monster game?
VP of Human Resources: You make it up as you go along and then he'll tell you how you are doing it wrong.
Me: Oh, so it is the same rules as the marriage game!

Does anyone else have house rules for the marriage game?

#shewasnotamused #mayhavebeenslapped #daddydaycare #mycoworkers

### May 4, 2020

Coming into the break room wearing a mask that looks like it came from The Incredibles, a Superman cape, one black elbow-length glove, and an orange belt, our senior entertainment associate announced he would no longer be called by his name. He said, with a face as serious as Christian Bale playing Batman, "I am JumpDash. My sister's name is Cutes. Your name is Saves because you save *name of newest hire* from me a lot. My mom's name is AngryNice because she gets angry and nice sometimes."

#mommywantsadoover #idosaveheralot #daddydaycare #mycoworkers

### May 6, 2020

Before our morning shift began, my coworkers decided they wanted to go on a socially distanced vacation inside our office. They drug their "suitcases" (not sure if they realized they were simply sleeping bags or if that's how their family packs) full of children's toys around the second-floor executive offices. I may have to administer a "random" drug test because one told me we had arrived at our beach house, which was actually the office of our VP of Human Resources, and proceeded to dump the 15-20 pounds of toys from his "suitcase" in the middle of the floor. Then he asked me to help him pick them up!

#nowheismadwedidntplaywithhistoys #thenerveofthisguy #spiritoftravel #daddydaycare #mycoworkers

Update: He then arranged said toys into a long train from our VP's desk to the storage closet. Picture edited to protect the innocent.

### May 7, 2020

Going to have to write up one of my coworkers for defacing company property. Not sure if it'll come off. I couldn't find the SDSs (Safety Data Sheets) for this product. Upon reading the labels of these writing instruments, I am going out on a limb that they are expired because the writing instrument said it "was hable." Google determined that this is an antiquated term for being "generally able or handy" or, if it was used in a nautical setting, "an old seaport or haven."

#iamnotcleaningitup #spellinghumor #51stinteruptiontoday #daddydaycare #mycoworkers

### May 7, 2020

Words I never thought I would ever have to write on an HR incident report: "Please stop climbing through the basketball hoop net." We may have to install signage and have departmental training. One coworker's actions may just ruin it for the rest of us.

#commonsense #wheredidthelisteningearsgo #daddydaycare #mycoworkers

### May 8, 2020

Today, one of my coworkers is obsessed with taking pictures. He has taken his camera around the office to snap pictures of nearly everything in sight: Lego creations, other coworker's feet, stairs, pillows on the couch, etc. While not normally an issue, he has one of the older cameras where you hear the shutter beep. After about the 40th picture in the span of a minute and realizing he was not taking his time to compose a photo, I asked him to politely stop. He looks at me timidly, smiles ever so slightly, and hits the button again.

#hemaylosethatfinger #someofushavetowork #notasingleselfie #daddydaycare #mycoworkers

## May 11, 2020

I think of myself as pretty easy to get along with and understanding. According to my coworker, I am not fair. While conducting an audit of one coworker's accounting skills, he broke down in ugly tears when I told him we were adding up the inventory and not sorting it by colors. On the plus side, he did pass the three questions I asked him before the meltdown...

#wewerecountingpompoms #craftsupplyfail #daddydaycare #mycoworkers

## May 12, 2020

Do anyone else's coworkers play Whose Line Is It Anyway during the day: "Where the games are made up and the points do not matter"?

Apparently, flipping a stuffed Mini Mouse onto a mess-free drawing board with the butt touching the board is worth 50 points but landing your toss of said mouse in a sitting position is worth zero points.

First, who knew this was a game? Second, I am sure even Drew Carey would throw a challenge flag on the point system my coworker invented.

#anythingisagame #bigbabywhenheloses #daddydaycare #mycoworkers

### May 13, 2020

While I was on a late-in-the-day conference call, one of my coworkers came strolling into the room I was in. While paying attention to something else, I notice him walking away with something off about the situation out of the corner of my eye. In nothing but a t-shirt, he announces loudly that he needed to take both his pants AND underwear off because they got wet. He casually sits down in another coworker's office chair and acts like nothing is wrong. Thank goodness I was on mute because I had to go off on him for violating...well...everything. I told him we would set up a meeting when my call was finished to determine when we could discuss his Personal Improvement Plan.

And it was then that I realized I was a terrible person. No one should have a meeting about setting up another meeting. Period. The. End.

#atleasthewaszoomready #toomanymeetings #whatdayisit #daddydaycare #mycoworkers

### May 15, 2020

On the one day I have taken off in the past few weeks, our youngest associate shows up, bright-eyed and bushy-tailed, for work at 5:45 am. She is now wearing a toy baby crib as a hat. Even if we had something addressing head coverings in the uniform policy, I doubt she'd be granted a religious exemption.

#cantcatchabreak #theforceisstrongwiththisone #daddydaycare #mycoworkers

### May 15, 2020

In other uniform news, I politely asked our senior entertainment associate to put his on before starting our shift. When I came back to check on him, he was sitting in a ball pit in the break room. When I issued him a verbal warning, he stared at me with an intense angered gaze, as if he was trying to shoot lasers through his eyes at me. He then immediately proceeded to pick up one of the balls in the pit, maintaining his devilish glare, and licked it in obvious defiance. It was then that I knew today was a lost cause for productivity.

#nosleepforthewicked #wearenotinthistogether #prayforhim #daddydaycare #mycoworkers

### May 16, 2020

I feel like it is commonplace at work to have that one coworker who constantly talks, is a "know it all", or is just generally disruptive or annoying. I bet you have one of these people working with you and have dreamed of the day you could put said coworker in a box and tape it shut. I am here to tell you I have lived the dream and it was as magical as you could've imagined.

#bestthreesecondsofmyday #shouldveusedstrongertape #daddydaycare #mycoworkers

### May 18, 2020

We are at the "Get your legs out from under the rug!", "Do you know the mustache man?! Because I am! Because I am!" (to the tune of the muffin man), and "Can I smell you?" point of our day and it is not even 10 am.

#atleasthehasashirton #mondayweirdos #daddydaycare #mycoworkers

### May 19, 2020

Sprung for breakfast for my coworkers this morning. Rather than being thankful for the gesture, do you know what one of them told me?!

"I am not eating this toast! It is not flat enough!"

All Blues Brother's references to dry white toast are appropriate.

#iwillflattenyourattitudedude #spoiledbrat #daddydaycare #mycoworkers

### May 19, 2020

We had to get creative with budget cutbacks since this whole thing started. Office security came up as an area to save some money temporarily. During today's brainstorming session, one of my coworkers volunteered to serve as a guard. When I told him he needed PPE, he confidently told me he would take care of it. He also, of course, had to have a special title. So, I present to you, our new head of security: "Red Power Ranger."

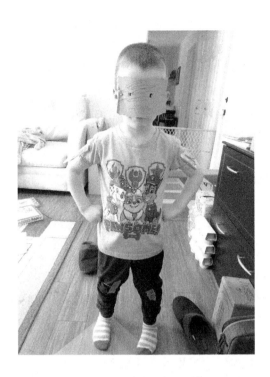

#heforgottoletthemarkerdry #brightredface #daddydaycare #mycoworkers

### May 20, 2020

While discussing dinner options en route to pick up our VP of Human Resources from her remote office, one of my coworkers chimed in with, quite possibly, the best idea he has had all month. He was singing it too so he gets bonus points for creative adaptations of a childhood classic. "Do you know the taco girl, the taco girl, the taco girl? Do you know the taco girl who lives on Glenridge Drive!"

#hedoesnotliketacos #hehadnuggetsinstead #everyoneneedsatacogirl #daddydaycare #mycoworkers

### May 21, 2020

Things have gotten so bad in the labor market that now anyone is trying to get inside for an interview. This guy was tapping on the back windows for more than 3 hours yesterday and is now back at it this morning. Give the guy points for persistence. I have notified our current staff of the need to maintain quotas if they intend to keep their jobs.

### May 23, 2020

In either a feat of strength or stupidity, one of my coworkers broke the door to the break room oven. I am thinking I should still file paperwork to have her pay docked for a replacement, as it does not seem repairable. Her only saving grace is that it hasn't heated anything correctly in years. On the other hand, I am mildly intrigued/impressed she was able to only break the bottom hinge and not the top.

P.S. For those of you who know my coworkers, I hope you enjoy that reference in the third sentence.

#microwavemealsforher #shehulk #daddydaycare #mycoworkers

### May 24, 2020

I feel like our office has descended into a bad game of #madlibs. I personally said the following statements to both of my coworkers tonight, all in the span of about 60 seconds:

1) Please stop licking the door.
2) Why are you karate-chopping a submarine?
3) Did you really just lick my t-shirt?!

#releasethebeasts #isittheweekendyet #nowiknowwhymomsdrinkwine #daddydaycare #mycoworkers

### May 26, 2020

After a long weekend, one of my coworkers was visibly excited to come back to the office. While watching a TV show in the break room before his shift began, he explains to the entire team, "I am so excited! I am so excited that I am going to smack my booty butt." He then proceeded to commence with said action at least a dozen times before breaking out into a strange interpretive dance with several pelvic thrusts and hula hoop-looking moves. Hope he can keep the enthusiasm and creativity up for the next 8+ hours because I may not be able to match his level of excitement.

#mightypupsforinspiration #shouldibeconcerned #daddydaycare #mycoworkers

### May 26, 2020

Upper management may question my leadership after this one. The same coworker lost ANOTHER tooth while on the job. I know the optics on this aren't the best but, thankfully, no one was injured. First aid was applied and was proven effective. I did start an incident report to cover the organization and employee in case something comes up later. When I asked him what happened to cause the tooth to come out, he replied, "I bit the couch." At least we have the updated contract from Tooth Fairy LLC on hand from the last time. Should ease the procurement process this time around.

#dollardollarbillsyall #wigglewigglegone #daddydaycare #mycoworkers

### May 27, 2020

Our senior entertainment associate (S.E.A.) and I were conversing last night before calling it a day. This is the transcript of said conversation:

S.E.A.: What do you want?
Me: About 4 - 6 hours to myself.
S.E.A.: Nope, you get a sandwich.

#makeitadouble #canigetanopewiththat #dudeissavage

#daddydaycare #mycoworkers

## May 28, 2020

I am going to preface this update by saying, "I get it". Not everyone is gifted when it comes to the kitchen. But this was a head-scratcher:

*Senior entertainment associate comes out of break room looking confused and suspiciously sly at the same time*
Me, asking in a rhetorically irritated tone: Dude, what is that?
Employee: A spinner winner.
*Drops whisk on my desk and casually saunters off back to work*

#addwhisksavertomyresume #maybeitwasaheart #daddydaycare #mycoworkers

## May 29, 2020

This time, the "wow, thanks Captain Obvious!" comment did not come from my coworkers but from a member of the medical profession. Because one of my coworkers was not able to drive herself to the ear, nose, and throat doctor, I offered to take her. While at the appointment, the doctor said, and I quote, "We have seen a big decrease in ear infections since this pandemic started."

#alldolledupwithnowheretogo #35dollarcopayforthat #brilliant

#daddydaycare #mycoworkers

## May 31, 2020

I know deconstructed food is a hot trend in the culinary world. Taking a traditional dish and breaking it up into individual parts to create something new is both creative and fun. However, I do not think that is what my coworker had in mind when she successfully removed the cheese from inside her cooked quesadilla. I mean, she picked it off so cleanly that you wouldn't even know it was at one point a cheese sandwich on a tortilla.

Meanwhile, our senior entertainment associate has sour cream in his hair. That should explain itself.

#boredeater #pickyandthebrain
#atleastheisusinghiscarrotchompers #daddydaycare #mycoworkers

## June 1, 2020

One of my coworkers is using the creative side of his brain today. When asked to create something that would help our office be more productive, these were his words:

Senior entertainment associate, gesturing towards a cushion on the couch: "I created a 'trampoline sender.' I jump on my trampoline here and it sends me to a nap!"

For anyone who has ever fallen asleep on the job, I have identified the narc.

#ihelpedcreatethisbrilliance #heisnextlevel
#trampolinesenderforrent #daddydaycare #mycoworkers

### June 1, 2020

Our senior entertainment associate just delivered this gem. While sitting at the lunch table before the third shift came in, I heard him talking softly to himself while staring lovingly at something on the table:

S.E.A.: Can I drink you? *baby giggle sounds* Tickle tickle tickle!
Me: You know you can get your own.
S.E.A.: Nope, I was just teasing her water bottle.

Does anyone have a policy on harassment of inanimate objects I could use as a benchmark when updating our policy manual?

#whohiredthisguy #didthebottleflirtback #daddydaycare #mycoworkers

### June 2, 2020

Need advice on a possibly reportable HR issue. One coworker was seen lying inside the laundry hamper for uniforms in the middle of the hallway this morning. She was mumbling incoherent words and phrases like a child and was fairly unresponsive to requests to move. I conducted an informal sobriety test, which she passed. Her breath smelled like milk so I am wondering if she used it to cover up for something else. Other than this brief incident, she has been productive and listens to instructions. Should I call her emergency contact on file to advise of the issue?

#wasshemilkdrunk #hertherapistrecommendedavacation #daddydaycare #mycoworkers

### June 3, 2020

We all have said stuff we regret, right? Well, our senior

entertainment associate is single (and not ready to mingle) so I must apologize to whomever he may date in the future for sharing something he may regret saying a few years down the line:

"I just tooted in my face. I ripped my butt apart and put it back together."

#thebuttofthejoke #herippedaripeone #massevacuation #daddydaycare #mycoworkers

### June 4, 2020

I am amazed at the way some people, who call themselves professionals, handle themselves. I am currently watching an argument between two coworkers over a stuffed animal one had on her desk. You would think a simple verbal request would suffice to get him to return the stolen property. What did she do instead to get him to comply?

What any reasonable person would do, of course: throw a first aid kit at him!

However, she missed a perfect opportunity to yell, "you are going to need this!", before chucking it at him.

#sanitizethisdude #redcrosswontsaveyounow #bandagebandit #daddydaycare #mycoworkers

### June 5, 2020

What was your "I knew I worked with aliens" moment? I just had mine today when I witnessed our company's newest hire do this to her mid-shift snack.

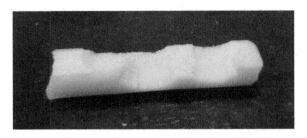

#pollyohnoshedidnt #mozzarellamurderer #daddydaycare #mycoworkers

### June 8, 2020

After a healthy-turned-heated discussion over what was on the menu for lunch, my coworker and I agreed to disagree about what we were going to actually eat. What sparked this discussion you ask? First, it was "the cheese on the quesadilla was not cut right." When I offered to go behind the counter and make my coworker something else (rookie move Mike...rookie move), he then said, "the meatballs are too hot", and refused to cool them off himself. He decided it was in his best interest to take the rest of the afternoon off as unpaid leave yet refused to leave office premises.

I know I have mentioned before that we serve a FREE workplace-provided lunch to all employees. Anyone else have a good story of coworkers who complained about something and you still came out on top?

#whereswaldo #excusethemess #beachofficenextweek #daddydaycare #mycoworkers

### June 9, 2020

Every place I have worked has had that one coworker who shares a little more than you care to know. The streak continued here when one of my coworkers shared this little ditty just before shift change last night:

"I am going to go upstairs and poop. You watch my (Fig) Newton. I am not done eating it!"

Curious to hear any over-sharing stories others may have...

#RegularRy #hisfuturegirlfriendisgoingtohateme #daddydaycare #mycoworkers

## June 10, 2020

While discussing cleaning methods for the office prior to next week's mandatory PTO for all employees, our senior entertainment associate gave this suggestion, while holding up the remote control to the break room TV:

"We should get a Tooter gun! Pew, pew, pew!"

I am hoping he was referencing those electrostatic sanitizing sprayers and not an actual fart gun like in the movie Despicable Me.

#filthyanimals #canyousanitizehisattitude #askingforafriend #daddydaycare #mycoworkers

## June 11, 2020

I think my "mandatory PTO for all employees next week" announcement backfired. Two of my coworkers are demonstrating a complete disregard for order and politeness. One coworker put herself in the workplace-provided luggage, tried to hide a fork in a pillow, and is now spinning another coworker around and around in an office chair. Our senior entertainment associate has kissed the biceps of our newest hire, called me a cupcake, and is now belly-flopping on pillows in the corporate offices. Pretty sure HR is going to move up his P.I.P. completion date after today's incidents.

I sure hope this vacation fixes their productivity and communication skills because it is sheer chaos in here.

#letthemgoletthemgo #cantholdthemdownanymore #daddydaycare #mycoworkers

### June 13, 2020

SABOTAGE! When I said mandatory PTO for all employees, I did not mean we all had to go to the same place! Our senior entertainment associate and newest hire snuck into the car this morning so guess I do not get a break from their antics. And since it is a road trip to get where we are going, they insist on only eating McDonald's while on the road. So guess who had McDonald's for the first time in years...

#canigetanumberNOPE #happymealshappyemployees #daddydaycare #mycoworkers

### June 15, 2020

During an intense game of Uno this morning, our senior entertainment associate stopped the game during his turn and announced, "Excuse me, I need to scratch my butt.

"#washetryingtocheat #discretionisnothissuperpower #daddydaycare #mycoworkers

### June 16, 2020

I was sitting on the couch minding my own business when our newest hire came over to me. She opened up my hand and placed some goldfish crackers in it. Confused, I asked her if they were for me. She smiled with an ear-to-ear grin, bowed her head, and ate the goldfish out of my hand like a baby bird.

#birdfeederforhire #freshoutofseed #daddydaycare #mycoworkers

### June 17, 2020

That feeling of victory when I tell our senior entertainment associate to go pound sand and he actually follows the instructions to a T!

#justneededsand #surehelistensnow #daddydaycare #mycoworkers

### June 20, 2020

We had just pulled away from our lodging for the week when our senior entertainment associate asked us to turn around. Wondering what he had forgotten, we asked him why. He said, in a manner that could only be described as humorless and serious, "I forgot to hug the top bunk, bottom bunk, and the TV."

In proper management style, we acknowledged his contribution but...

#wekeptondriving #hehasneverhadabunkbedbefore #hugginginanimateobjectsfor200Alex #daddydaycare #mycoworkers

### June 22, 2020

Firmly positioned at the bottom of most job descriptions is verbiage to the effect of: "and other duties, as assigned." Today's assigned "other duty", you ask? Picking rainbocorn poop out of my coworker's hair because he was trying to be a Teenage Mutant Ninja Turtle by wrapping it around his head, in the middle of his shift. Do you have an odd "other duty" story to share?

#rainbocornwasnotinventedbyaparent #newagesillyputty #itisEVERYWHERE #daddydaycare #mycoworkers

### June 23, 2020

I am writing up our senior entertainment associate for failure to abide by personnel policy 14.2-1a: "All employees must wear appropriate attire for their position at all times." He is currently running in circles topless, as fast as he can, in the break room. He's yelling, "I am as fast a cheetah!!!", and I am just sitting here waiting for him to finish so he can sign his acknowledgment of his ever-expanding P.I.P. form.

#wearenotatthebeachdude #whensoapmakesyourshirtwet #daddydaycare #mycoworkers

### June 23, 2020

Not to be outdone, our newest hire went into the community kitchen for what seemingly was a snack break. While I was on a video conference call, I saw her bent over the office dog's water bowl, swishing around a Paw Patrol band-aid and shouting, "All clean!"

Not thinking to hang up from my Zoom call, we reviewed

handwashing procedures together while everyone else looked on as if nothing unusual was happening (or at least they were polite enough to not say anything). I thanked her for her attempt at recycling but told her budget cutbacks hadn't gone to THAT extreme.

#whobredtheseanimals #marshalldidnotneedabath #fakebooboosfortheloss #daddydaycare #mycoworkers

### June 24, 2020

Interviewer: What is your biggest strength?
New hire: I have a hunger for knowledge.

This is a PSA to remind everyone to ask clarifying follow-up questions during your interview process. Otherwise, your newest hire will literally be eating the pages of books while on duty. Speaking from experience having watched this unfold a second ago...

#boardbookstastelikecardboard #devourabookIRL #daddydaycare #mycoworkers

### June 25, 2020

Hearing a slight rustling in the community kitchen, I felt the need to investigate, especially when one of my coworkers was making a clanging sound with his voice. When I peeked around the corner, I witnessed our senior entertainment associate and newest hire battling it out with...drum roll, please!...cheese stick wrappers. After asking them what was going on, our S.E.A. said in a very nonchalant manner, "We were playing with trash swords."

#nocheeseleftbehind #homiedontpeelthat #daddydaycare #mycoworkers

## June 26, 2020

One of my coworkers did not agree with a decision I made this morning. Rather than have a healthy discussion about it, he said, "you are going to jail!" When he ran back to his cubicle, I thought he'd come back with the phone in hand and the police on the other end. Nope...

#pleasesendhelp #atleastihaveafacecovering #sociallydistantapproved #daddydaycare #mycoworkers

## June 29, 2020

When I came home with food from our VP of Human Resource's favorite restaurant the other day, one of my coworkers took offense that he did not get anything. Irate, he threw a temper tantrum and screamed, "You get an X. You get an X [referring to our VP]. I get a check. You know why? Because I am the garlic knotter. The garlic knotters eat all the garlic knots!"

#iwanttobeagarlicknottertoo #didhegivememoney #nexttimeorderahead #daddydaycare #mycoworkers

### June 30, 2020

Casually sauntering away from the executive offices, our senior entertainment associate uses his best Jim Carey impression (think The Mask) and says, "Did someone order take out?!" He then sprints down the hallway and shoulder checks our newest hire, immediately sending her to the ground. Thankfully, she was not harmed and refused to file a report.

Admittedly, I laughed quite hard because his delivery was ON POINT! However, I was fully aware I had to serve him his inappropriate conduct paperwork so HR doesn't report me.

#shelaughedtoo #orderedamisconductsandwich #comedianintraining #daddydaycare #mycoworkers

### July 1, 2020

Of course you oblige when your peevish coworker asks you to wrap him up like a burrito. Despite not knowing what actual work-related project this pertained to, I felt it was justified for the betterment of morale for the entire office.

What I did not expect was our new hire to actually attempt to consume said human burrito. She went after him like it was taco Tuesday.

#breakforlunch #wraphimupforsafety #picodeNOyo #daddydaycare #mycoworkers

## July 2, 2020

While discussing our plans for the day over lunch, our senior entertainment associate stated, in a very quiet and somber time, "Sometimes I have to lay down and scratch myself when I get itchy." Not wishing to violate HIPPA regulations, I did not ask him what condition was causing his "situation" but suggested he take the rest of the afternoon off to try to feel better.

#notcaptainsubtle #sirscratch #daddydaycare #mycoworkers

## July 3, 2020

My coworkers' meltdown moments so far today have been brought to you by:

- not understanding how to successfully place four discs in a row on a grid.

- being asked to wear a uniform/not be naked.
- participating in a mandatory team bonding exercise.
- having a fake sword desk ornament removed from his workspace for failure to maintain proper decorum with management.

In other perplexing news, our newest hire was seen sucking on the antenna of a work-issued walkie talkie so there's that...

#nowtheyreflushingtoiletsforfun #thosewereuglytears #isitquittingtimeyet #daddydaycare #mycoworkers

### July 5, 2020

Just minding my own business, going to the supply closet to get something. What do I find? Our newest hire sitting on the floor with what looked like Elsa gloves on, brushing the hair of a pair of Teenage Mutant Ninja Turtles. When I asked her what she was doing here on a day off, she got mad, screamed "No!", and slammed the door closed in my face. It is at this point I am seriously regretting giving my coworkers the building codes...

#iwilltakeitdoesntbrushfor100alex #letitNoletitNo #turnsoutyoureallycantholdthembackanymore #daddydaycare #mycoworkers

### July 6, 2020

One of my coworkers silently decided to paint me something this morning. What she neglected to share was that her canvas would be the walls in the break room and her medium would be fig bars. So now our office looks like someone literally threw poop on the wall...

Should I write her up for defacing company property, participating in unapproved activities during business hours, or something else?

Happy birthday to me *my shocked face goes here*

#figsinflat #birthdaybrown #thankfullyitwashedoff #daddydaycare #mycoworkers

## July 7, 2020

"First, you put bread on the bottom. You can't put the cheese on next because the turkey goes on top of the bottom bread. The cheese goes on the turkey and another bread on top. So it is bread, turkey, cheese and bread. That's how you make a turkey and cheese sandwich." I haven't felt talked down to like this in ages. Considering restricting our senior entertainment associate's purchasing account as a consequence of the belittling behavior. What say you?

#notmyfirstsandwichrodeo #ditchhiswich #ispeanutbutterandjellynext #daddydaycare #mycoworkers

## July 7, 2020

After I am done feeling so belittled over how to make a turkey and cheese sandwich (literally 2 minutes later), I look over at our newest hire while in the lunchroom. Oblivious to the fact everyone else was watching her, she was stuffing green beans up her shorts. Went right on eating when she realized we were all glaring at her in disbelief.

When everyone was done with lunch, our newest hire and senior entertainment associate stared at each other with sweet smiling faces. Then the more senior of the two employees shouted, "Do you want to go burp with me? Let's go burp together!"

#daisydukesdonthidemuch #whyaretheysogross #mouthfartexperts

#daddydaycare #mycoworkers

## July 8, 2020

Everyone has their way of getting excited about being assigned a project, coming up with a great idea, closing a sale, or a goal being met. Some people, like me, do a little fist pump or shout "YESSS!!" out loud while others do it quietly to themselves.

With that being said, our senior entertainment associate was very excited when I suggested he be assigned to the satellite office down the street for a few hours today. His response? "Dino charger ready! Energize! Unleash the power! Now I feel dino charged!" Hand motions and body flailing were included in his demonstration of excitement.

#asimplethankyouwoulddo #zordonwouldbehanginghishead #gogopowerdelegation #daddydaycare #mycoworkers

## July 9, 2020

Just when I thought we could make it through ONE whole day without some ridiculous comment or deed by our workforce, karma rings the doorbell and yells, "Gotcha!"

As we are getting ready to clock out (in a dead silence I should add), our senior entertainment associate swings around quickly and whispers, "Did you hear that?!... I call that a ghost toot..."

#wesayheistoosavage #tootermansavednoone #mighthavechokedalittlebit #daddydaycare #mycoworkers

## July 10, 2020

Y'all, we lost a beloved member of the office today. Colorful, extremely flexible, always open for hugs and handshakes. We had a moment of silence to honor the loss. There were ugly tears and a lot of sobbing, mostly by our senior entertainment associate who was close to the deceased.

You had a great life, Mr. Squishy Orbeez ball. All 3 days we had with you were filled with fun and water.

#hulksquish #nomessisfakenews #mandownandoutofstock #daddydaycare #mycoworkers

## July 11, 2020

To enhance my understanding of different cultures, is sucking the nose of your coworkers a sign of endearment or respect in any other country? If not, I think my coworkers may be trying to thread a very thin needle on our company's behavior policy. I would hate to have to write a "Keep your tongues to yourself" policy. Seems rather redundant...

#slobberslobbereverywhere #nothingissafe #theyarethereasonthereisapolicyforeverything #daddydaycare #mycoworkers

## July 13, 2020

I have heard of people calling out "sick" and seen coworkers hiding where security cameras can not see in order to get out of doing their job. In that light, I think my coworkers may not have screwed in their lightbulbs correctly today when they decided to hide under the rug in the break room.

However, given the state of the country at the moment, I am thinking I may need to invest in them more, given their creative skills. They may be onto something here which the rest of us have overlooked.

#wheredoyouthinkyouregoing #freakingnowhere #wheresspot #daddydaycare #mycoworkers

### July 14, 2020

On a scale of "Dude, it is fine" to Ludacris' "Roll Out", how concerned should I be for our business when our VP of Human Resources asks one of our employees on a daily basis, "Where are you and do you have pants on?!"

#timetomonsterdotcomthesefools #canronajustgetoveritselfnow #timeforashortsale #daddydaycare #mycoworkers

### July 15, 2020

Anyone have a personal hygiene policy I can review? Thinking I may need to implement one after our recent company outing. We were on our way to drop off a package when our newest hire was spotted in the rearview mirror doing something unsanitary. I know, I know. you are probably thinking she was picking her nose, scratching her butt, or something more common.

Nope. She took her sandal off and used it to scratch her nose. There was nothing else in her hands.

#solesister #isawblackgunkonthebottom #barf #daddydaycare #mycoworkers

## July 16, 2020

I have certainly heard about drinking on the job and the negative impacts it has on the employee and their colleagues. However, I do not think there has been enough scientific research on taking shots of fig bars while on the job.

Nothing in policy 1.14-c says our newest hire should receive corrective action but maybe HR should connect her with a behavioral physiologist or perhaps an addiction counselor? Any other suggestions?

#firststepisadmittingyouhaveaproblem
#healthyishselfcareforthewin #shediddrinkthefirstone
#daddydaycare #mycoworkers

## July 17, 2020

Time to call out the indecisive people in your life. This happened in the cafeteria for breakfast this morning:

Senior entertainment associate: I will have melted butter toast
*Chef turns around toward kitchen*
S.E.A.: No, wait... I will have toast with butter.
*Chef, irritated, starts to prepare said order*
S.E.A.: No, make that regular toast.
*Chef, starting to fume, walks slowly toward toaster*
S.E.A.: On second thought, I will just have plain bread.
*Glaring, the chef hands him the whole loaf*
S.E.A.: Thanks! I am a bread-eating machine!

#wholewheathassler #justpicksomethingalready #youhavehadthemenuformonths #daddydaycare #mycoworkers

### July 19, 2020

With our VP of Human Resources picking up custodial duties and sweeping directly in front of our senior entertainment associate, the tenured employee says, "You know who makes the most mess? HR! I will save you from the evil mess-making HR lady!"

In the immortal words of Stephanie Tanner, "HOW RUDE!"

#hesaidmommybutHRladyfitbetter
#iwillsweepyouintonextweekdude #shouldathrownthebroomathim
#daddydaycare #mycoworkers

### July 20, 2020

While helping our newest hire with a uniform change due to lack of sufficient job experience, she came up to me with the most genuine and endearing gaze, waving her finger at me like a sassy grandmother, and said what nobody in the room was thinking:

"No bite ducks!"

#lifeadviceyoudidnotknowyouneeded #futurePETAmember #brakeforbeaks #daddydaycare #mycoworkers

### July 20, 2020

Can anyone else relate to having that one coworker who overhears EVERYTHING?!

*Our newest hire reaches into my personal cabinet of food in the kitchen*
Me: Hey! Stop manhandling my bread!
Senior entertainment associate, storming into the kitchen from the opposite end of the office in a rage of fury like the apocalypse was happening: Did you just call her a rainy head?!

#surenowhelistens #daddydaycare #mycoworkers

### July 22, 2020

I think my coworkers were baiting me by being well-behaved and respectful employees yesterday. "Why?" you ask? Because our newest hire shows up to work, seemingly mocking the dress code, with what could be best described as "if you blindfolded Rafiki from the Lion King and gave him a blueberry colored makeup brush"

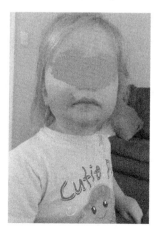

#hakunamatatalifestyle #blendingneedswork
#thisiswhywwedontgiveherhardtasks #daddydaycare
#mycoworkers

### July 23, 2020

During our company meal prior to shift change, our senior entertainment associate pokes our VP of Human Resources in the arm. Annoyed by the uncalled-for physical contact and with her sandwich still in hand, she glares at him and he delivers this gem:

Do you wanna know what you are?
*Insert 3 second pause for dramatic effect*
An EATasaurus!

In a non-pandemic environment: time of termination: 6:34 pm.
In a pandemic environment: heavy eye roll and asked to not reference anyone's eating habits.

#bitemecorona #doyoutalktoyourmommawiththatmouth
#HRsaidnotolettinghimgo #daddydaycare #mycoworkers

### July 24, 2020

This pandemic has a lot of folks rethinking their business and careers. During a conversation in the lunchroom, we were discussing career options if we had to do things over. Not hesitating, the first thing our senior entertainment associate says is this: "No one wants to be a toilet seat. Then people would sit on you and put poop in your mouth!"

#crappyjob #isthatdegreefromPU
#probablymybesthashtagyet #daddydaycare #mycoworkers

### July 25, 2020

While asking my coworkers for creative ways to motivate the team, our senior entertainment associate says this, in the most genuine way possible:

"Do you want to play the cry game? The one where you go into your bed and cry?"

#whataretherulesofthisgame #firsttotearswinsorloses #iwasthinkingcatchphrase #daddydaycare #mycoworkers

### July 27, 2020

In today's D.Y.K. tear-off calendar: did you know you can accurately and quantitatively measure the level of effort an employee is putting into his or her work by simply referring to pictures of them, captured randomly throughout the day?

What? You do not believe me?

#irestmycase #sheisnoweatingaplasticpikachu #motivationmonday #daddydaycare #mycoworkers

## July 27, 2020

We are all probably guilty of trying some kind of a seemingly odd or quirky remedy to improve performance or to look and feel better. Well, our senior entertainment associate came up to me this morning with a "sure-fire" way to increase his speed at work and wanted to share it with the rest of the company. Admittedly, I thought he was going to segway into the newest MLM scheme and ask to drop it in the employee newsletter. However, he showed me this bottle and said you can run "super-duper fast" when you put it on. Lathering himself up with clearly more product than necessary to demonstrate, he sprints down the hallway yelling, "Pikkkkaaaa....chuuuuuuuuuu"

Does anyone else have a remedy or product they swear by to improve productivity in the workplace?

#notthatkindofenergizing #shockingyetnotshocking #daddydaycare #mycoworkers

## July 28, 2020

I caught our senior entertainment associate off task, as well as being temporarily absent, this morning. When I confronted him about where he had gone, he said, "I was saving my sister from Snot Boy and my mom from the evil Dr. Biscuit!" Trying my hardest to contain my laughter at the ridiculousness of the situation, I fired back with this witty retort, "Was Dr. Biscuit's power a Super Butter Slather blaster?" With a stone-faced and stoic glare, he immediately replied, "Yes, how did you know?"

#hisliewasflakyatbest #ijammedhisplan
#pillsburynotasponsoryet #daddydaycare #mycoworkers

## July 29, 2020

You know it is a slow day at our office when the only funny thing said was the following:

Me: Hey, I could use your help on this. Can you come here?
VP of HR: I will be right there. I am currently fighting with another coworker over a sword.

#ithadlightsandsoundsbutstillasword
#givingsliceanddiceanewmeaning #daddydaycare #mycoworkers

## July 30, 2020

While conducting a research experiment on temporary absenteeism with my coworkers today, our senior entertainment associate FINALLY said something I can fully support:

"Ready or not, here I pickle!"

#cucumbersforthewin #toobadhedoesnoteatthem #moreforme

#daddydaycare #mycoworkers

## July 31, 2020

I refer you to my comments from four days ago about the level of effort assessment technique I discovered. When observing during a random spot check, you can clearly see my hypothesis is validated. The only fringe defense to the contrary is our newest hire was actually bobbing for M&Ms on the lunch table during her lunch break. At least she was putting effort into something…

#bobshergrandpa #hedoesfitintheboxnormally #newthemesonginthecomments #daddydaycare #mycoworkers

## August 2, 2020

This is a first. I have never witnessed a working professional put a pacifier in their mouth to calm themselves down in front of other coworkers before. After some brief research into why she was so distressed, it turns out that she was mad she couldn't get her nails done or have chocolate.

#firstworldproblems #icannotrelate
#shouldhavemadeahappyplate #daddydaycare #myvoworkers

## August 3, 2020

While developing a new marketing strategy for a new animal-themed kid's exercise program, I thought our team should put themselves in the mindset of the target audience. I volunteered to walk like a crab and our newest hire said she would move like a dog. What did our senior entertainment associate say he would be? He threw a blanket over his head to act as the shell, proceeded to start fake snoring, and quietly said, "I will be the turtle." A FREAKING TURTLE PEOPLE!

#maximumeffortminimumresults #dudeisnextlevel #feartheturtle #daddydaycare #mycoworkers

## August 4, 2020

My colleagues and I were working on a campaign for a popular children's modeling clay in separate workspaces. Suddenly, our senior entertainment associate comes storming into my office with only purple Mike and Ike candy in his hand. This was the exchange we had:

S.E.A.: I am making a new invention. it is a candy muffin!
Me: *scratching my head* So it is made out of candy and looks nothing like a muffin?
S.E.A.: Yep! Except now it is a transformer and it has a white booty

#patentdenied #itsallinhowyoumarketitdude
#maybeheisadecepticonIRL #daddydaycare #mycoworkers

## August 5, 2020

Should I be concerned about my safety and well-being when the words "Stop eating the paper towel roll" are directed to my coworkers?

#guessishouldfeedthem #istherefiberinpaperboard #whatdidicreate #daddydaycare #mycoworkers

### August 5, 2020

Honestly, I do not even know what our senior entertainment associate was doing when this incident occurred. Maybe it was an objection to an assignment. Maybe it was bickering over the lunch menu. Or maybe it was our newest hire breaking apart his meticulously put-together puzzles turned desk decor. Whatever it was, he was screaming the following quote at the top of his lungs. You could hear what he was saying from the second-floor executive offices with all the doors closed:

"WHY DO I HAVE TO DO THINGS OVER AND OVER?! I had to crawl over *name of our newest hire* a thousand times and now she has the ball on fire."

#becauseweallovedoovers #noextinguisherswereneeded #obligatorygreatballsoffirereference #daddydaycare #mycoworkers

### August 6, 2020

I thought I had really accomplished something y'all. I was led to believe I was receiving a recognition only bestowed to those who have done something above and beyond the call of duty. At least that's what my coworker led me to believe from the certificate he gave me. During an informal ceremony, he presented me with one of the three keys to the city. When I realized he said the key was to "the kingdom of thedooruh", I hung my head and walked away.

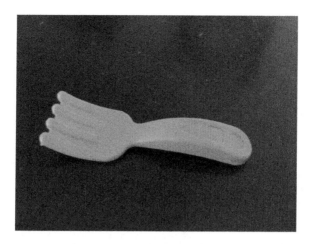

#budgetcutbackonkeys #forksforfakers
#aretheothertwokeystomoredoor #daddydaycare #mycoworkers

### **August 7, 2020**

Never have I ever:
- witnessed a coworker hugging a power line pole
- watched a coworker view a daily safety video with sunglasses on
- had to physically separate two coworkers after uttering the words, "stop beating him with that eggplant!"

Until today…

#areeggplantsontheTSAapprovedlist
#thesunneversetsonabadass #polehuggerbutnotlikethat
#daddydaycare #mycoworkers

### August 9, 2020

Name-calling in politics has become part of that culture, unfortunately, but I had hoped it would not bleed over into corporate America. I witnessed this sad transition today when our newest hire was arguing with our senior entertainment associate. The unprofessional behavior she demonstrated, being almost three years his junior, was uncalled for. While chasing him down the hall over a disagreement about a child's baby doll which she had been using as a stress reliever, she hollered, "Get back here booty butt!"

#babygotback #hegotwhathedeserved #daddydaycare #mycoworkers

### August 11, 2020

Last night, the 3rd shift meal was plain cheese quesadillas. While not inherently a messy food, there was a minor mishap with our senior entertainment associate. Sitting at his assigned seat without a shirt on (goodness knows why...), some sour cream fell off the cheesy sandwich and onto...well...you'll see...

S.E.A.: mmm, look, belly cream!

#thatisonehappybelly #atleasthedidnotapplyitlikelotion #ole #daddydaycare #mycoworkers

## August 12, 2020

It was quiet. Too quiet. So I went downstairs to investigate why my coworkers were being so abnormally silent. Hoping to see them hard at work at their desks, I was appalled at what I saw. While I know our company provides a lot of perks not afforded to other organizations, I specifically remember saying no to complimentary pedicures during work hours.

Yes, my friends. That's our senior entertainment associate picking the dead skin off of the feet of our newest hire.

#pedisurethatisgross #whatrhymeswithphalanges #theyarealwaysunderfoot #daddydaycare #mycoworkers

## August 12, 2020

I think our senior entertainment associate does not know the difference between scary and heartwarming, or how video/audio works. This has me questioning his ability to provide proper judgment in the workplace. While discussing The Good Dinosaur, a Disney movie:

VP of HR: That movie makes me sad.
S.E.A.: Then next time watch it with your eyes closed.

#seenoevilyetcanstillhear
#healsowearsheadphoneswhilevacuuming #daddydaycare
#mycoworkers

## August 13, 2020

Just heard the truest thing our senior entertained associate has said since he transitioned to this office. While skipping/running down the hallway of our second-floor executive offices, he screams, "BULL IN A CHINA CLOSET! BULL IN A CHINA CLOSET!"

The same coworker, three minutes later: "WHY won't anyone let me in the quiet game?"

#TheTruthShallSetUsFree #canigetanamen
#toneitdownthursday #daddydaycare #mycoworkers

## August 15, 2020

Not even 20 minutes after yesterday's heartfelt message, my coworker decided he needed to share his feelings on the topic of people blowing hot air for others to hear. Being the apolitical type, this was rather strange for him. He politely raised his hand to indicate he had something to share and said the following in a quiet and confident tone, "Excuse me. I need to burp in your mouth."

#atleasthewaspolite #filthyanimalgotfunnies

#politicalsatireforthewin #daddydaycare #mycoworkers

## August 16, 2020

Great! There's bound to be a financial audit in our future. Ugh!

We spent the allocated "employee morale" budget this month on our senior entertainment associate's birthday today. But one of our finance managers discovered that our VP of Human Resources also purchased a "sympathy gift" for our newest hire. When other employees hear they did not get a gift, it is going to be dreadful for productivity. Talk about office politics! So much for this year's balanced budget...

#herpoutgameisstrong #onesuckertwowinners #whybotherwithabudget #daddydaycare #mycoworkers

## August 17, 2020

Apparently, there must have been a typo in the company-wide memo I sent out, entitled "Personal grooming of others and the health and safety risks it causes."

Our VP of Human Resources had stepped in some paint earlier today, which had not been placed in a job-appropriate location (investigation still ongoing as to why). While taking a break in the employee lounge later in her shift, her propped-up feet must have acted as some kind of distress signal because our senior entertainment associate dashed right over to try to pick the dried paint off for her. I do not know whether I am more disturbed by his attempt at picking at her feet or that she allowed him to do both feet.

#yallnasty #saynotothetoe
#whoactuallywritescompanymemosanymore #daddydaycare
#mycoworkers

## August 18, 2020

In our office, disagreements happen frequently. Instead of sending scathing, behind-the-back, emails to colleagues to complain about another coworker, we settle things like professionals.......

With lightsaber battles in the dark in the hallway leading to our executive offices. Sure, there may be some yelling and a lot of made-up sound effects but at least no one leaves mad at their opponent *ahem* I mean coworker.

#jedisnotjargon #unleashyourdarkside #imayhavehitalittletoohard #butidontregretit #daddydaycare #mycoworkers

### August 19, 2020

I know I am not supposed to ask about an employee's health status but I am starting to get concerned about our newest hire. I think she may suffer from "Selective Limb Usage Syndrome." Today, during our lunch break, I saw her bend her head over her plate and lap the ranch dressing up like she was a dog over the water bowl. This is not the first occurrence either. Last night, she went bobbing for Goldfish over a bowl of snacks during her allotted 15-minute break. To notify her emergency contact or no?

#bobshergrandpa #HRcalledthedoctorandthedoctorsaid #nomoremonkeys #daddydaycare #mycoworkers

### August 20, 2020

It was like time was moving in slow motion right before my eyes. I could see the carnage about to take place. The vindictive look on our senior entertainment associate's face, expressing his disdain for upper management, was piercing.

After we had politely asked him to perform a work-related task, he flexed his muscles, extended his arm, and gave the universal sign all middle schoolers know all too well but I have never seen used in a professional setting before: "talk to the hand." I am surprised he still has his appendage.

#homiedontplaythat #lethimgolethimgo #canyoukaratechopyouemployeeslegally #daddydaycare #mycoworkers

## August 21, 2020

Our senior entertainment associate asked me a serious question that I felt compelled to answer with as much poise as I could muster:

S.E.A.: Why does nobody laugh at my jokes?
Me: I am not sure chief. Maybe you could share one of your jokes?
S.E.A.: Sure. Knock, knock.
Me: Who is there?
S.E.A.: Home.
Me: Home who?
S.E.A.: When am I going home so I can have an exploding sandwich?

#crickets #nowonderitbombed
#sorrytobreakittoyoubutthatisterrible #daddydaycare #mycoworkers

## August 22, 2020

Because our employees' P.I.P. required it, our VP of Human Resources was giving a refresher presentation to our employees today on office expectations. The topics of respect, communicating with others while displaying a positive attitude, and even office cleanliness were covered. However, she had to stop during the presentation to point out what everyone else in the room was seeing happen with our newest hire during the working lunch: "We are not table lickers!"

#nopastanoodleleftbehind #iworkwithanimals #whatwouldyoulikeatablefor #daddydaycare #mycoworkers

## August 23, 2020

I am not sure if our VP of Human Resources is about to turn in her two weeks notice or practicing her routine before applying for the next season of *America's Next Top Comic*.

Quote of the day: "I do not care if there is a spotted leprechaun zebra out there. Y'all need to calm it the heck down."

#peaceoutwitches #datsfunnyrightder #soitisnotjustme #daddydaycare #mycoworkers

## August 24, 2020

Can someone help me understand why hide and seek is not used more in team-building activities? I feel like no one in corporate America uses this technique to build employee engagement. It is especially useful for motivating underachieving employees. Do not believe me?

Try sending your most bothersome employees to go hide. They get a positive feeling of accomplishment and develop creative thinking skills. Meanwhile, you get the 5-10 damn minutes of peace and quiet you deserve as you sit down, do not look for them, and randomly yell, "Nope, they are not in here."

#winning #teambuildingtakessacraficeyall
#ivolunteerastribute #daddydaycare #mycoworkers

## August 25, 2020

So I am minding my own business in the lunchroom when our senior entertainment associate saunters in with nothing but his underwear on. At this point, I just ignored it, thinking there's a likely explanation coming.

As I turn to eat, he runs back to the break room and I hear him giggle and say, "Go ahead and put the stickers on me." Sure enough, I then see him lying on the couch like one of those art models you'd see in college and our newest hire is plastering him with random stickers. Suggestions on writing this one into the policy handbook?

#stickysituation #whyisheconstantlyinastateofundress
#whereistheeasybuttom #daddydaycare #mycoworkers

## August 26, 2020

I will have to check our project management system again because I do not recall any government contacts coming in lately. We are a creative marketing and education company so I was surprised when I saw my coworker spending time on a contract for weapons development. He neglected to let his supervisors know about this new market segment he wanted to enter. Maybe he's onto something with this new invention though: "the biggest blaster ever."

#whereismy20percenttime #clearlyexceededscopebudget #senditbacktoRandD #daddydaycare #mycoworkers

### August 26, 2020

I am admittedly a yes or no, follow the rules, look at the instructions, kind of person. So I would like to share my method for organizing and managing my workspace:

Step 1: Identify the problem area.

Step 2: Develop a solution to reduce strain and automate as much as possible.

Step 3: Implement a system so the likelihood of the problem reoccurring is greatly reduced or eliminated.

Or if you prefer visual, step-by-step, IKEA-style instructions, see below.

#myisocertificationlevelisexpert #managinglikeaboss #whenindoubtputitinthelaundry #daddydaycare #mycoworkers

### August 28, 2020

After the dress code issue from earlier this week, I thought I would be helpful and offer our senior entertainment associate a hand with staying compliant. Noticing something off about his appearance, here was our exchange:

Me: Hey, there's something in your hair.

S.E.A.: I hope it is not that rainbocorn poop again.

#whywasheworkingwithpoop
#turnsoutunicornsdoexistanddopooprainbows
#canttheworldjuststaysavedforaminute #daddydaycare
#mycoworkers

### August 29, 2020

We work to foster a place of creativity and health in our office. So it came as a surprise when I heard the sounds of someone snorting. I am not talking about the "you are laughing so hard you cannot control it" kind of snorting if you catch my drift. The sounds were fairly consistent in timing between snorts and were followed by big inhales of air.

With my phone in hand about to dial 911, I come into the break room and find the culprit doing the deed. Who knew the training manual we gave our newest hire was a scratch and sniff edition? Oh, she was chasing her scratch and sniff sessions by licking the scented dot on the page. Guess I should've read it too...

#addictedtothesniff #shouldweinformthepublishertheyareenabling #atleastsheopenedupthemanual #daddydaycare #mycoworkers

## August 30, 2020

I noticed our newest hire was sticking her tongue out more than usual this morning. Thinking she may be hot, I ignored it. Unfortunately, I found out why a few minutes later when our senior entertainment associate spilled the beans to explain her temporary behavior situation...

"Hey, do you want to play lick tag with us?"

#stilldoesnotexplainwhythecouchhadwetspots #iseeourmedicalpremiumsgoingupsoon #hardpass #daddydaycare #mycoworkers

## August 31, 2020

Our newest hire may have tried to contact the publisher of the now-infamous training manual. I checked her call logs and did not see anything I recognized. However, they must've sent her a sample of an upcoming release because I saw her, unabashedly, licking the cover of a book this morning while on a company outing.

Being a helpful coworker, our senior entertainment associate speaks up and warns her, "Hey, if you do not stop that you will get a book burn!"

#nicetrybucko #thankfullyitwasnotmydraftcopy

#iamgoingtoneedatherapist #daddydaycare #mycoworkers

### September 1, 2020

My theory is you can successfully guess someone's age by the number of times they have gathered random items throughout the office, rewrapped said items, and given them to themselves since their last birthday. If my theory holds, our senior entertainment associate is 59 years old.

It has only been 16 days since his last birthday...

#hecomplainedaboutwhathepickedout #excessiveamountoftape #regifterrescue #daddydaycare #mycoworkers

### September 2, 2020

So let's start with the end first: That sweet, sweet feeling of victory! Albeit at the expense of someone else's discomfort...

We recently announced that the risk department is now strictly enforcing a no-running policy in all indoor spaces (outdoor jogs are still encouraged). I go downstairs to the break room for a drink and hear the quick patter of feet from the second-floor executive offices above me. The running sounds were quickly followed by a GIANT thud. Smiling to myself because I knew exactly what happened, I heard our senior entertainment associate yell, "Ow! That hurt! But at least I got him in the skittle!"

#tastetherainbowofitoldyouso #eatitandweepsucker #myguiltshoweduplateforlaughingathim #sorrynotsorry #daddydaycare #mycoworkers

### September 3, 2020

Ever have coworkers show up for work almost two hours early at 5:20 am? No one had even turned a light on yet. Our senior entertainment associate woke our VP of Human Resources up, who had slept at the office due to an ongoing project, and announced he had already used the restroom. I guess that's better than going elsewhere...

We tried to send him home but he refused to go so here we are. I foresee a lot of breaks being needed today to keep him from hitting overtime and veering off task.

#prayforus #aflushstarttotheday #doesheevenclockout #daddydaycare #mycoworkers

### September 3, 2020

Our team went on our morning walk to keep the creative juices flowing. Most folks would grab their water bottle, fitness tracking device, or phone, right?

Not our team...Yes, my friends, my coworker grabbed a broom...

#bippityboppityboo #heaintplayinquidditch #wantedtosweepawaypuddles #daddydaycare #mycoworkers

### September 4, 2020

Does anyone have tips for how to deal with office romances? Our newest hire brought a flower back to the office and placed it on the desk of our VP of Human Resources. I am pretty sure she's smitten and doesn't know how else to express herself.

Not sure whether to intervene and tell her it is a dead dandelion weed or to let things play out...

#whenbudgetcutshithard #waitingnotdatingseason #whytheygottabesavagelyweird #daddydaycare #mycoworkers

### September 6, 2020

Despite his verified telephone competency and comprehension of the English language, our senior entertainment associate insists on screaming across the office to communicate. we have hired consultants, used progressive discipline, and had many one-on-one discussions. I am mildly concerned he may not appreciate the position he is in with our company.

However, today he demonstrated his appreciation for our office team:

S.E.A., again screaming across the office: Hey, *insert name of VP of Human Resources*, can you come down here?
V.P.: Sure, why?
S.E.A., still screaming: I just want to see you!

#hashenotfiguredoutzoomyet #maybehehasacrushtoo #alittlebitvinegaralittlebitsugar #insidevoicesplease #daddydaycare

#mycoworkers

### September 7, 2020

I think our senior entertainment associate misses the outside world. He brought a giant, 6 foot, folding, pillow bed into the break room (where did he hide this thing in his office?!) and laid it down on the floor. He proceeded to use it as a combination conveyor belt and barcode scanner with boxes he re-gifted to himself...

#heusedtherealbeepsounds #itisbarely7am
#ifyouareboredicangiveyoumoreprojects
#daddydaycare #mycoworkers

### September 8, 2020

After working with people for a few years, you begin to learn a lot about them in both a professional and personal way. Some things are typical such as favorite foods, music, and places they like to go and other bits of info are, well, not. I guess you can see where this is going...

Yesterday afternoon during a fleet maintenance trek, I learned that our newest hire is scared of...drum roll, please!

Drive-thru car washes.

Not only was she shaking in the backseat but she was also covering her ears and yelling, "No like car wash!"

Can anyone else top that?!

#sherepeatedthatatleast63timesafterweleft
#uniforncolorsdidnothelp #longesttwominutesoftheweek
#daddydaycare #mycoworkers

### September 9, 2020

Working in our office summed up in one sentence:

Saying "Can you please stop licking the metal bench?" at least 3 times while your other coworker is randomly yelling "PICKLES!" at the top of his lungs in the background.

#wishiwaslying #nowiknowwhyconsultantscostsomuch #isitquittingtimeyet #daddydaycare #mycoworkers

### September 10, 2020

I would like to report a hiring policy violation. Our senior entertainment associate told me he recently hired a new employee. I did not, nor did other members of upper management, authorize said hire so I was rather irate at his decision. He clearly ignored the hiring freeze we implemented 2+ years ago (a pre-COVID mandate).

He pleaded his case by saying he already loved her and would take her around everywhere he went (purportedly for training purposes?!). The only thing I knew about her personally or professionally is that he called her Bun Bun.

It turns out Bun Bun is the stuffed squeaky toy our office dog buried at the bottom of her toy box years ago. He clutched onto Bun Bun all morning as they ran around the office, even throwing a fierce pouting episode when he dropped her on the floor. So there's that...

#capitaloffense #howdidshesqueakbyHR #theanswerisinsomeoneshands #onlytimeitisokaytothrowcoworkers #daddydaycare #mycoworkers

### September 11, 2020

We hold a strict no-smoking policy in our office. We haven't had to put up signs because our intake training on this topic is very successful. This morning, I was taken aback when I saw our newest hire with something resembling a cigarette in her mouth. As I marched across the office to pull it out of her mouth, I figured it was one of those new-age designer ones: a bright blue color with a neon orange tip.

As I pulled it out of her mouth, I felt both dumb and perplexed at the same time. Y'all, she was chewing on a Nerf dart.

#notasponsorbutwishtheywere #nerfwar #nerfisnotagatewaydrug #putthatinyourpipeandsmokeit #daddydaycare #mycoworkers

### September 12, 2020

For comedy hour at our office, here's the only highlight of our senior entertainment associate's stand up routine:

S.E.A.: Knock knock.
Me: Who's there?
S.E.A.: Shark.
Me: Shark who?
S.E.A.: I am always hangry.

Yes, that was his best joke...

#canigetanamen #eatingmachine #hungrynothillarious #daddydaycare #mycoworkers

### September 12, 2020

Ever get the feeling you are being watched? Well, I had just poured myself a bowl of tortilla chips to snack on. Hearing nothing behind me and that creepy feeling of being spied on, I glanced over my shoulder and saw our newest hire pointing at the bowl of chips with one finger and the other one scratching her nose. Figuring she wanted some, I walked over to give her one.

As I offered the crispy morsel to her, she proceeded to grab my hand and wipe the boogers she had on both fingers on my hand.

#donotorderherguac #passingthepinkypico #daddydaycare #mycoworkers

## September 13, 2020

Our coworkers swore to me that they had superpowers. Laughing out loud, I said, "You do, eh? I gotta see this!"

Our newest hire flexes her arms, places her hands on the break room table, and moves it 3 inches. Trying to outdo her, our senior entertainment associate makes a revving sound and sprints across the room, despite his written and verbal acknowledgment of our no running policy.

Except he slipped on a sleeping bag HE brought to the office and face planted on the ground.

#karmasogoesoof #thatwillteachhim #theirtruesuperpowerispestering #daddydaycare #mycoworkers

## September 14, 2020

In today's, "well, do it your damn self then" moment of zen, I was assisting the kitchen staff with lunch service. After sitting down for his lunch, our senior entertainment associate brings his plate back to the counter, in tears. Asking him why he was upset, he responds with, "Because my cheese is too wrinkly."

#thereisareasonitiscalledcheeseproduct #makeyourownsammiethen #itallgoesdownthesamepiehole #daddydaycare #mycoworkers

## September 15, 2020

So we got a grant to do some deferred maintenance on the outside of the office. While the contractor was pressure washing the building, our senior entertainment associate volunteered to act in the supervisory role to ensure contract compliance.

When I came to check on the progress, he pointed out the window with the beaming eyes and smile of a child on Christmas morning and shouts, "Look, he's got a poop canoe!"

#hewasreferringtothesprayer #hopeitdidnotcrapoutonhim #iseevocabularytraininginhisfuture #daddydaycare #mycoworkers

### September 16, 2020

I feel like I can safely assume we have all had some WEIRD conversations with our coworkers. Some are rather mundane while others border on recommending seeking professional medical advice...

Well, while our team was having a working lunch and discussing upcoming projects, our senior entertainment associate randomly interrupts and screams at the top of his lungs, "Catapult, stegosaurus, fire apple!"

#isthereatakehometestfortourettes #thanksfortheheadsup #undersiegebyaprehistorictree #daddydaycare #mycoworkers

### September 17, 2020

With all this renewed focus on deferred maintenance at our office, I was excited to have the entire team's buy-in on these important projects. Our newest hire was even doing her best to help where needed.

Recognizing that the furniture had not been polished in a while, she took it upon herself to start this maintenance all by herself! I even gave her a big shout-out in front of the team during our morning meeting.

However, I had to have a private discussion with her about

referencing the MSDS to ensure they are compliant with the surface she is applying the product. Y'all, she used lip balm on our senior entertainment associate's uniform locker...

#smellslikevanilla #captainchap #daddydaycare #mycoworkers

## September 18, 2020

Asking what your coworkers do for fun outside of the office is a pretty common question, right? I was not expecting to be given a full-on demonstration by our coworkers of their "talents." I present to you, my part-time comedians:

S.E.A.: Knock knock.
Me: Who's there?
S.E.A.: Chicken nugget.
Me: Chicken nugget who?
S.E.A.: Chicken toots!

Newest hire: Knock knock.
Me: Who is there?
Newest hire: Booty butt.
Me: Booty butt who?
Newest hire: Stinky goblins feet.

#pleasestopencouragingthem #comediansinfailing

#dontlaughchallenge #daddydaycare #mycoworkers

## September 19, 2020

Our VP of Human Resources has been stepping up to help clean the office while the purchasing and finance departments continue to mull over how and when to select a new vendor. Between meetings this morning, she did a pretty good sweep of a lot of smaller items.

Then our senior entertainment associate strolls through all of the downstairs spaces she had just cleaned and offers up this observation, "Hey, how did this place get so clean?"

#surprisedheisstillemployed #stopcontributingtoityoufilthyanimal #daddydaycare #mycoworkers

## September 20, 2020

There is always that one song that comes on the radio or preferred streaming service that gets you pumped up or moved in such a way as to get you singing it at the top of your lungs. For those who want to know, my jam is Plastic Cup Politics by Less than Jake.

Well, our newest hire was also moved by a song today. With her office door swung wide open for all to hear, her eyes closed, and laying flat on the floor, she belted out this memorable hit: "Bye-bye poopies. Bye-bye poopies. Bye-bye poopies, we gon' send you away!"

#billboardnottop100 #whatacrappychorus #whenyourbowelsaremovedtoo #daddydaycare #mycoworkers

# **Note of Encouragement**

I started to share my coworker antics to give my friends something to laugh at amid all the uncertainty this pandemic has presented to everyone. This is a slight departure from that goal but one that I still hope gives you something positive to think about and a glimmer of hope.

While on the phone with my dad and out of the blue, he tells me, "I know it is hard and you are doing your best. If there was anyone I would vote on to make it through all this, it is you. I love you and keep on keepin' on."

I want you to know that, since you are reading this, I vote for you to make it through this time too. Stay positive, find something to laugh at (even if it is your bothersome coworkers who do not have boundaries), and smile. You can do more than you think you are capable of.

#yesyoucan #cameforthelaughs #stayedforthefriends #mycoworkers

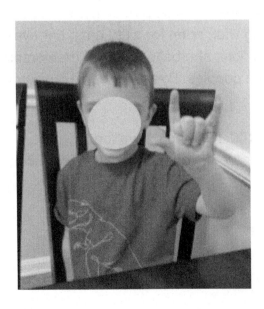

## **Special thanks to:**

A: Your continuous support means more than words can describe. Also, please put away your uniforms.

R & G: Thanks for making me pay attention to the small things. You are the reason this was possible.

Dad: Your constant belief in me means the world.

Deena and Nicole: For sharing your editing skills with me.

You, the reader: Thank you for believing for at least one second that these were my actual coworkers.

## **About the Author**

Mike Stoupa is a tourism sales professional with a distinct sense of humor. A graduate of Virginia Tech's Hospitality and Tourism Management program, Mike is a proud father of two questionable coworkers and a could-be-better husband. If you have any questions for Mike, fire away because there is no such thing as a stupid question until he tells you otherwise…and to date, he's only had to tell that to one person.

You can reach Mike via email at authormikestoupa@gmail.com and can follow him at www.Facebook.com/AuthorMikeStoupa.

## A final note from our CEO

I want to first thank you for deciding to indulge yourself in the comedy of horrors that was my COVID-19 experience at the "office." The struggle was as real as the stories. I hope you laughed so many times that you forgot about your own COVID-19 experiences for a minute.

As such, if you found this book to be a useful or questionable distraction, I would greatly appreciate it if you would leave your feedback where you purchased your copy so other people know what they are walking into. If you also feel so compelled, sharing the book with your friends, family, and coworkers on your social media accounts would mean others could share in the comedy.

Thank you again for your time and attention. May your future work-from-home setup be a dumpster fire-free zone and void of any policy violations.

Made in the USA
Middletown, DE
23 December 2021